US Women's
NATIONAL
SOCCER TEAM

FRISCO, TX SHEBELIEVES CUP PRESENTED BY VISA MA

US Women's NATIONAL SOCCER TEAM

Winning On and Off the Field

Heather E. Schwartz

LERNER PUBLICATIONS ◆ MINNEAPOLIS

This book is dedicated to my soccer star BFF Jenna Lisella.
Thanks for getting me through gym class!

Lerner Publications Company
An imprint of Lerner Publishing Group, Inc.
241 First Avenue North
Minneapolis, MN 55401 USA

For reading levels and more information, look up this title at www.lernerbooks.com.

Main body text set in Rotis Serif Std.
Typeface provided by Adobe Systems.

Editor: Brianna Kaiser **Designer:** Lauren Cooper

Library of Congress Cataloging-in-Publication Data

Names: Schwartz, Heather E. author.
Title: US Women's National Soccer Team : winning on and off the field / Heather E. Schwartz.
Other titles: U.S. Women's National Soccer Team
Description: Minneapolis, MN : Lerner Publications, [2024] | Series: Gateway biographies
  | Includes bibliographical references. | Audience: Ages 9–14 | Audience: Grades 4–6 |
  Summary: "From over 500 wins to star players, the US Women's National Soccer Team is
  exceptional. Learn about the team's history, their records in the FIFA Women's World Cup and
  the Olympics, and more"– Provided by publisher.
Identifiers: LCCN 2022055466 (print) | LCCN 2022055467 (ebook) | ISBN 9781728491752
  (library binding) | ISBN 9798765602959 (paperback) | ISBN 9781728497587 (ebook)
Subjects: LCSH: U.S. Women's National Soccer Team—Juvenile literature. | Women soccer
  players—United States—Biography—Juvenile literature.
Classification: LCC GV944.U5 S45 2024 (print) | LCC GV944.U5 (ebook) | DDC 796.3340973—
  dc23/eng/20221214

LC record available at https://lccn.loc.gov/2022055466
LC ebook record available at https://lccn.loc.gov/2022055467

Manufactured in the United States of America
1-53114-51124-2/27/2023

TABLE OF CONTENTS

The USWNT celebrates after winning the 2019 FIFA Women's World Cup.

By halftime, the 2019 FIFA Women's World Cup final grew tense. The US Women's National Soccer Team (USWNT) hadn't scored a single goal. Neither had their opponent, the national team from the Netherlands. Then, in the 61st minute of the game, it happened. As more than one billion viewers watched around the world, US forward Megan Rapinoe slammed a penalty kick into the goal. At Parc Olympique Lyonnais, in Lyon, France, the crowd in the stands screamed with excitement. The US took the lead!

Megan Rapinoe (*front*) scores on a penalty shot during the final match of the 2019 Women's World Cup.

Minutes later, Rapinoe's teammate Rose Lavelle raced down the field, cut left, and took her shot. It was another goal for the US! She leaped into her teammates' arms as they hugged in celebration. By the end of the game, the score was 2–0 and the USWNT had its record fourth Women's World Cup win.

Fans were ecstatic. All around the world, they clapped and cheered their support. They chanted for the team and for equal pay. Everyone knew this team was fighting for more than just victory on the field. They were playing for a better future for female athletes everywhere.

Building the Team

Long before the USWNT formed, female soccer players organized to participate and compete in the sport. When about 70 women joined the Craig Club Girls Soccer League in 1950, they made history in St. Louis, Missouri. The players formed one of the best-known early women's soccer leagues in the US. Divided into four teams—the Bobby Soccers, the Coeds, the Flyers, and the Bombers— they competed in 15 games each season, drawing hundreds of fans who came to watch and cheer.

The playing conditions for the women's teams were worse than for the men's teams. Sometimes the women's teams played in bad weather while the men's games were canceled. The women's teams often had to improvise for equipment. They borrowed men's boots and stuffed magazines into their socks to use as shin guards. But they kept showing up and playing their best, with more at stake than just winning.

Many doctors at that time believed women were too weak to play sports. They even believed a myth that athletics could cause a woman's uterus to fall out, preventing them from having children. By succeeding in the sport, female soccer players were proving critics wrong and showing what they could do as athletes.

But by the 1960s, women were still being left behind in sports. There were no athletic scholarships for female college students. There were no championships for women's teams. Female athletes didn't always have the facilities and equipment they needed because funding for sports went to men's teams.

Women who were serious about sports, and soccer in particular, also faced limits beyond college. Women's soccer wasn't an Olympic sport. There weren't many national teams in the world. And there was no path for female soccer players in the US to play professionally.

In 1972 only 30,000 women participated in National Collegiate Athletic Association (NCAA) sports compared to 170,000 men. And there were not as many women's teams as men's teams. That year Title IX was passed. It prohibited discrimination based on sex in schools and other federally funded programs.

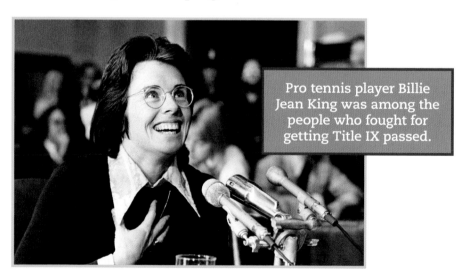

Pro tennis player Billie Jean King was among the people who fought for getting Title IX passed.

Also in that year, the Gertrude Dudley Scholarship became the first nationally advertised four-year scholarship for female athletes. More funding went to women's teams at colleges. In 1982 the NCAA started Division 1 women's soccer.

The world was waking up. In 1985 the US Soccer Federation, often called US Soccer, got an invitation for female soccer players to compete in a tournament in Italy. Suddenly, a national team was needed. Players were selected during the National Sports Festival, a mini-Olympics-style competition for amateur athletes, in Baton Rouge, Louisiana. The players were surprised when they learned what was happening.

A USWNT practice in 1986

"After the last game, they sat everybody down and said, 'We're going to pick a national team and the team is going to train in New York and then you'll go to Italy,'" five-time USWNT player Ann Orrison said. "That was the first anybody had ever heard of it."

Along with Orrison, sixteen women from all over the US made the cut. As promised, they went to New York City with their coach, Mike Ryan, and played in scrimmages against local Long Island teams. After just three days, the team was scheduled to fly to Italy for the tournament. They were a team of strong players. But they were far from ready.

PAPER TEAMS

Before 1985 rosters for US women's national teams were formed from 1982 to 1984. Players were chosen from regional tournaments, and their names were put on a list. But they never played any games.

The Early Years

The members of the new USWNT didn't have much time to practice together. They didn't have official uniforms to play in either. The night before they were set to leave for Italy, they received a box from US Soccer. Inside were shorts, shirts, and pink-and-blue sweatsuits, all sized for men. With no time to spare, the players set to

Players compete at the National Sports Festival, later renamed the US Olympic Festival.

work cutting, sewing, and hemming the pieces.

Late into the night, they made the clothes fit. But they couldn't change the colors, which were wrong for a US team, and nobody had numbers to wear. It was time to travel. Ryan hauled a bag of soccer balls onto the plane, and the team took off.

At the tournament, the competition was fierce. The US took on Italy, Denmark, and England. The team didn't win any of the four games they played, but they tied with Denmark in one match. Although they had a losing record, the opportunity to compete in an international tournament made history and was a win for female athletes.

"We were just so happy to be there," forward Margaret "Tucka" Healy said. "While watching the Denmark–Italy game, we grabbed an Italian flag and rushed to the sidelines, where we led a cheer. They were totally shocked that we'd cheer another team."

In 1986 the women's team got a new coach: Anson Dorrance, who was head coach of the women's soccer team at the University of North Carolina. He set out to find the best players in the country to round out the roster. The national team was so new, even top players at the state and regional levels didn't know much about it. But Dorrance soon found several future stars of the sport, including Mia Hamm, Julie Foudy, and Brandi Chastain, who joined the team in 1987, 1988, and 1988, respectively.

Mia Hamm (*left*) with coach Anson Dorrance during a practice at the University of North Carolina

In its second year, the team had its first home series in Blaine, Minnesota, and won two out of three games against Canada. They also played at the tournament in Italy again and racked up victories against Brazil and China. April Heinrichs, the team's first captain, scored five goals and was chosen as the US Soccer Female Athlete of the Year in 1986.

FINDING MIA HAMM

When Dorrance heard about a talented 14-year-old playing soccer for the North Texas regional team, he flew there to see for himself. Though no one pointed her out to him, Dorrance knew right away which one was Mia Hamm. She was that great on the field. When she joined the national team at 15, she became the team's youngest member.

With a national team, women's soccer was blazing a new trail. The team was packed with talent, drive, and passion for the sport. When FIFA hosted its first women's tournament in 1991, they were ready to prove themselves.

Once again, women had to overcome sexism in sports. FIFA was willing to host a women's tournament, but the organization wasn't prepared to call it a World Cup, a title then reserved for men. Instead, they named the event the 1st FIFA World Championship for Women's Football for the M&M's Cup. They also shortened matches from 90 to 80 minutes for female players. And the conditions were far from glamorous for the USWNT.

"We're staying in these dumpy hotels, and we're hearing about the men's team staying in these nice hotels," Foudy said. "And we're getting $10 a day and no salary."

The USWNT was up against more than just their competitors at the tournament. But they focused on their immediate goal, dominating in all six matches and winning the inaugural Women's World Cup.

"We had a mentality that we weren't going to lose and we were going to fight," said midfielder Shannon Higgins-Cirovski. "If you would've compared us player for player, we might've been a bit more athletic, but it was really our mentality."

Julie Foudy (*center*) playing in a match at the 1st FIFA World Championship for Women's Football for the M&M's Cup.

The event was a victory for the US, a turning point for female athletes, and a milestone for women's soccer. But barely anyone knew about it. The games weren't broadcast, and the only way players could let their families know about their success on the field was by faxing them the news. On the flight home, some of the players sat with the captain. They had milk and cookies together and told their stories.

When the team arrived home, no crowd of excited fans greeted them—only their bus driver and operations person met them at the airport. "We were not famous. No one knew we existed," goalkeeper Kim Wyant said.

They still had a lot to do if they wanted to prove themselves as serious soccer players.

Fighting for Equality

After the FIFA win, US Soccer rewarded the women's team with notes of congratulations and a $500 bonus for each player. The men's World Cup was supported by about $50 million in prize money. But the women were excited to be paid at all.

"I thought, '*Whoa, this is incredible*!' And now when I look back and tell this story today, people are like, '*That is horrible*,'" Chastain said. "And it *was* horrible, to be honest, in hindsight. But in that moment, I remember thinking how lucky we were, because I didn't know anyone who was doing what we did on the national team to make money."

The USWNT continued playing, scoring major victories along the way. In 1994 they won the Chiquita Cup—an international tournament where four teams compete—led by a new coach, Tony DiCicco. By 1995 they were preparing for a history-making competition. Women's soccer would be represented for the first time at the 1996 Atlanta Olympics. The players were thrilled at the opportunity not only to compete but to show up for young fans, who looked up to them and saw a path for themselves.

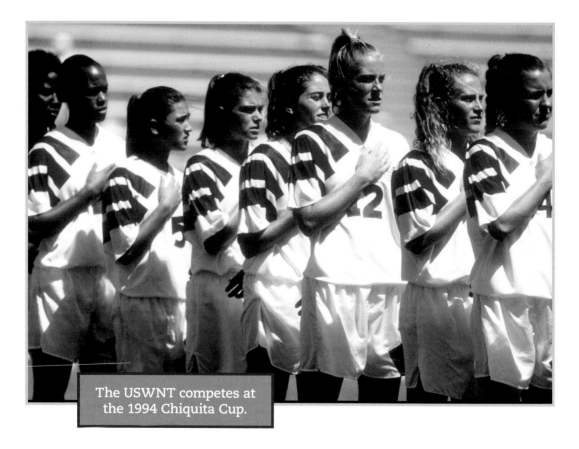

The USWNT competes at the 1994 Chiquita Cup.

"I dreamt of being an Olympian ever since I was 6 or 7. I always knew I wanted to be part of the Olympics, and I had such conviction about it," said forward Shannon MacMillan.

Shannon MacMillan plays in a match at the 1996 Olympics.

"For these younger generations to have these powerful, confident females to look up to and realize the Olympics are a possibility, it was exciting. Now they had something tangible to hold on to as well as having the dream."

In 1995 the USWNT got its first sponsor: Nike. The company found them a permanent place to practice at the Seminole County Sports Training Center, in Sanford, Florida. Their new home base had six fields, a weight room, a big-screen TV, two locker rooms, nine tennis courts, and six racquetball courts.

It was a big leap forward for the women's team. But they struggled with pay inequities. While top male soccer players in the US earned more than $60,000 a year, top female players were paid much less: $25,000 to $40,000.

By the time the women were training for the 1996 Olympics, they had more power to demand what they deserved. When they saw their contracts for the Olympics, they realized male soccer players were once again getting a better deal. The men would be paid a bonus for any medal win: gold, silver, or bronze. US Soccer was willing to pay the women's team a $250,000 bonus if they won gold. But they offered no bonus for silver or bronze.

Michelle Akers, Joy Fawcett, Julie Foudy, Carin Gabarra, Mia Hamm, Kristine Lilly, Carla Overbeck, Briana Scurry, and Tisha Venturini took a stand. The nine players rejected their contracts. In return, US Soccer locked them out of the training camp that was scheduled to begin. The players were terrified. Some were convinced they'd lost their shot at the Olympics. But they all knew they were doing the right thing.

Midfielder Lilly remembers telling Foudy, "I don't know. I'm really scared that I won't play in the Olympics. And [Foudy's] like, 'Well, I am too. But this is gonna make a difference.'"

Powerful people at US Soccer weren't happy. But within weeks, the players got what they wanted. Their contracts included bonuses for any medal win at the Olympics, plus other demands they'd made: paid parental leave, paid nannies for players with children, and more. Encouraged by their victory, the women were soon back to training, determined to make their country proud.

Going for Gold—and More

By the time the players traveled to Atlanta to play in the Olympic Games, they were big news. They knew they had to protect their mental health as well as their physical health if they were going to win. A sports psychologist and other staff helped them keep their focus.

The team played in matches that drew an increasing number of fans. More than 25,000 people gathered to watch the team win their first match against Denmark. More came when they beat Sweden next. At the third match, 55,000 fans showed up to cheer on the USWNT. Their last match was against China, and they were going for the gold. When more than 75,000 fans showed up, it was the biggest crowd for a women's athletic event yet.

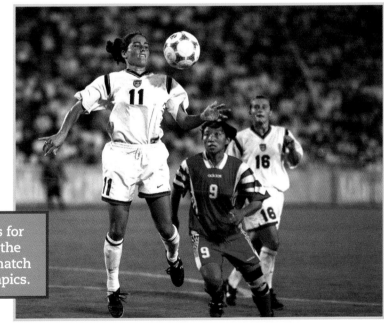

Foudy (*left*) goes for the ball during the USWNT's final match at the 1996 Olympics.

In the last 22 minutes of the game, Hamm passed to Fawcett. Fawcett set up forward Tiffeny Milbrett, who scored the winning goal. Working together, the USWNT won gold in the first-ever Olympics to include their sport. Screaming, laughing, and crying all at once, the women were overjoyed to win. And they were thrilled that they were growing the game for female soccer players everywhere.

The USWNT stands with their gold medals at the 1996 Olympics.

"When we played, we played because we loved it and because we wanted . . . to be the best in the world," Akers said. "But we also played to grow the game. We did that intentionally. And we played to inspire people."

The Olympic victory was a huge win for the US and for female athletes. But it was an exciting moment in sports history that many people missed when NBC didn't broadcast much of the game. Public outcry afterward proved people cared about US women's soccer. Their recognition of the players' talent and their desire to support the team was another triumph.

GROWING GIRLS' SOCCER

Many young players waited after games to ask members of the USWNT to sign autographs. The team helped girls see they belonged in soccer. By 1999 the sport was widely popular. The Soccer Industry Council of America reported 7.5 million registered female soccer players.

Soon after the team took the gold medal, FIFA announced the 1999 Women's World Cup would be held in the US. Organizers thought at first that the games should be in small stadiums. But they quickly realized they'd need the same large stadiums where the men's national soccer team played. Tickets sold out for the opening matches at Giants Stadium in New Jersey. The media decided to televise all 32 matches. Leading up to the competition, the players felt energized by the support they were getting.

"We want to show that we're excellent soccer players—smart, tactical, fit, fast, athletic—and we have everything the men's game has," Milbrett said. "We want respect."

Fans showed up in a big way for the Women's World Cup. As the team bus made its way through the city, players looked out the windows and saw tons of traffic. At first, they assumed people were there for a major event they didn't know about. They wondered what was going on. Then they saw cars that had been painted red, white, and blue. People were dressed in red, white, and blue too.

"They were waving at us and taking pictures. We were waving at them and taking pictures of them taking pictures of us," said Scurry. "It was amazing, because we went from, 'Oh my gosh, where are all these people going?' to 'We're going to be late!' to 'Oh my gosh, these people are here for us!'"

The players were shocked and excited. They were scared too. It was a strange experience. They'd been playing for years without getting much major attention.

Then they were the focus for a huge fan base. While they always played to win, the stakes felt higher with so many eyes on them.

Even though the team was rising, millions of people still didn't know about the Women's World Cup. The best way to get more notice for women's soccer would be to make the finals in the competition. The pressure was on, and some doubted they could rise to the challenge.

But the players were ready. "Tell us what we can't do and we'll do it. We love these types of obstacles," Foudy said. "This is the opportunity for us to show the world our sport and what we've done with it."

Winning the Women's World Cup

More than 78,000 fans showed up at Giants Stadium and watched the USWNT defeat Denmark in their first match of the 1999 Women's World Cup. As the tournament

Fans pack the Rose Bowl to watch the USWNT face China at the 1999 Women's World Cup.

continued, the team won five more games and made it to the final. Finally, they traveled to the Rose Bowl, in Pasadena, California, for a match against China that would determine the winner of the entire competition.

For the first 90 minutes, neither team scored. The game went into overtime. Midfielder Lilly leaped to prevent a goal by the Chinese team. Neither team scored during overtime, so the game went into a penalty kick tiebreaker. The crowd could not stop screaming and shouting for the USWNT and waving flags and signs as each player took their shot.

When Chastain got her chance to kick, she slammed the ball past China's goalkeeper into the net. The stadium went wild. Chastain tore off her jersey, waving it over her

head and sinking to her knees as her teammates raced onto the field. They'd won the Women's World Cup!

More than 90,000 people had packed the Rose Bowl to watch the game unfold live. And more than 40 million more watched it on TV. Afterward, the players were invited onto news shows. They appeared on the covers of *Time*, *Newsweek*, *People*, and *Sports Illustrated*. And they traveled to the White House, where they met President Bill Clinton and First Lady Hillary Clinton.

Such visible success could only lead to more good things for women's soccer, and very quickly, it did. In 2000 a group of media companies and investors started the Women's United Soccer Association (WUSA), pooling contributions of $40 million to launch the world's first women's professional soccer league. Eight US teams were in the league, and the 20 national team players were in too.

The league also drafted some of the best players from other countries, including China, Norway, and Brazil. The idea was to give top college players a place to play besides only the national team. They'd have opportunities to train and compete year-round. They would be paid to continue playing at a high level in their sport.

Another big change in women's soccer came when coach DiCicco stepped down after the Women's World Cup win. Player April Heinrichs, who had coached at every level and assisted DiCicco, became the national team's first female coach. With the 2000 Olympics on the horizon, she had a big job ahead of her. She also

April Heinrichs coaches the USWNT in 2000.

had a contract dispute to manage. Once again, the players were holding out for better compensation. Even after the Women's World Cup Win, US Soccer paid some players only $9,000 a year.

Their success on the field gave them more strength, and this time, they upped their demands, asking for better salaries, bonuses, and training facilities. Even President Clinton saw their point, and he pushed to pass legislation protecting equal pay for women and men. Still, US Soccer didn't want to give the players what they wanted. The organization claimed women's soccer only generated $1.6 million compared to $4.1 million generated by the men's team. But the women's team was performing better and drawing more and more support.

The national team players boycotted three games, refusing to play under an unfair contract. They needed to show they were serious about making change, not only for themselves but for future players. Before the Olympics began, the women finally got a new five-year contract. It raised salaries, offered bonuses for Olympic wins, and made other guarantees that satisfied the players.

"This is something we all believed in," Hamm said. "Some of us might be finished next year, the year after that, so this contract will outlive us."

Team Turnover

At the 2000 Olympics, members of the USWNT were determined to take home the gold medal. But pitted against Norway, they faced a shocking defeat. Even so, the team was happy with the game both sides had

THE NEXT GENERATION SCORES A WIN

Soccer for women continued to grow, with more opportunities for rising players. In 2002 FIFA organized the first-ever U-19 Women's World Championship for female athletes under 20. At the finals in Canada, the US won.

played. When they walked away with silver medals, they were proud. The *New York Times* described the competition as "one of the greatest women's games ever played, wide open and full of wild swings, breathless creativity, stirring defense, rapturous victory and inconsolable defeat."

Joy Fawcett (*left*) tries to get the ball before a member of Norway's team at the 2003 Algarve Cup.

After the Olympics, the USWNT won more matches, including the Algarve Cup and the Four Nations Tournament in 2003. They took third place at the 2003 FIFA Women's World Cup. And in 2004, they went back to the Olympics to battle for the gold again.

Mia Hamm, Julie Foudy, Joy Fawcett, Kristine Lilly, and Brandi Chastain— known as the Fab Five— would compete together for the last time. They played in 1,230 international matches and won the Women's World Cup in 1999. But Hamm, Foudy, and Fawcett had announced they were retiring after the Olympics, and Lilly and Chastain planned to retire soon too.

This time, the US women were up against Brazil in the gold medal match. Nothing about the game was easy. Many players on the Brazilian team were younger and faster. But the Fab Five still had talent, drive, and heart. And the US team had new superstars too, including Lindsay Tarpley and Abby Wambach, who scored the game-winning goal. As the women celebrated their gold medal victory, many saw the competition as a handing off of the team from the older founding players to the new generation.

Left to right: Julie Foudy, Joy Fawcett, Mia Hamm, Kristine Lilly, and Brandi Chastain sing the national anthem after wining the 2004 Olympic gold medal.

Over the next few years, the USWNT didn't have the big wins they'd scored in the past. But they were still contenders and in 2011, a competition forced the world to pay attention. At the Women's World Cup quarterfinals, a play by Wambach and Rapinoe pushed the US and Brazil into penalty kicks to determine the winner. Hope Solo's save at the goal and Ali Krieger's shot won the game and sent the US to the semifinals. They finished the Women's World Cup with a silver medal win.

The US team was soon off to the 2012 Olympics, in London, England. The gold medal match against Japan set a record by drawing a crowd of more than 80,000 people. Forward Carli Lloyd scored the game's only two goals. In the last five minutes, Solo made a save that ended the match, with the US taking the Olympic gold.

In 2012 the USWNT wins the gold medal for the fourth time.

The team continued to rise at the Women's World Cup in 2015. In the first five minutes, Lloyd scored twice. Not long after, she scored a third goal, making her the first player to achieve a hat trick at the Women's World Cup final. And the USWNT left with their first World Cup win since 1999.

Carli Lloyd (*front*) celebrates after achieving a hat trick, or three goals in one game, at the 2015 Women's World Cup final.

But while the next generation of top female soccer players was winning on the field, they were unhappy about the compensation they were getting. They knew they deserved better. The women's team was making more money for US Soccer than the men's team. Yet the pay structure was different for male and female players and the organization was still paying male players more.

"The numbers speak for themselves," Solo said. "[They] get paid more to just show up than we get paid to win major championships."

In 2016 five top players took action. Hope Solo, Carli Lloyd, Becky Sauerbrunn, Alex Morgan, and Megan Rapinoe filed a complaint with the Equal Employment Opportunity Commission, the US agency that enforces civil rights laws in the workplace. They were ready to fight for as long as it took to get equal pay.

Winning More Than Games

The USWNT knew their fans would support them. And they needed all the support they could get in their fight for equal pay. They launched a campaign, with Twitter hashtags such as #EqualPayDay and #somedayisnow. They wore T-shirts and temporary tattoos bearing the slogan, "Equal Play Equal Pay." They needed people to know what they wanted and why they were prepared to fight so hard. It wasn't great timing for the team. They were also getting ready for the 2016 Olympics.

"We would prefer not to have to deal with this," Rapinoe said. "But we're not going to shy away from it, either."

The team was excited for the Olympics, and in a match against Sweden, they battled for the win. When they lost, it was a huge disappointment. But that didn't mean the team's fight for equal pay was over. They still knew they deserved to be paid the same as male athletes.

By 2017 the members of the USWNT realized they needed to do more to get the agreement they wanted.

In 2016 a girl holds up a sign supporting the USWNT getting the same pay as the men's national team.

They hired new lawyers to help them negotiate with US Soccer. They got a new executive director for their union, the US Women's National Team Players Association. They also decided to create new leadership roles for players within the union. The team elected Becky Sauerbrunn, Christen Press, and Meghan Klingenberg to help lead the way. Other players joined committees and kept current, former, and future players in the loop.

"Our big goal is to have as many of the players cued in, and involved, and invested, as possible," Rapinoe said.

"That's something that can be really special about this."

By 2018 the team was performing better again, winning the SheBelieves Cup against England and the Tournament of Nations against Brazil. And in March 2019, they took things a step further in their fight for equality. The team sued US Soccer for gender discrimination. It wasn't just about pay. The women said the organization also showed discrimination in where they played, how they trained, their medical care and coaching, and their travel accommodations.

That summer the USWNT beat the Netherlands at the Women's World Cup. Many fans supported them, with more than one billion watching worldwide. Yet the women still hadn't reached an agreement with US Soccer about equal pay. The men's team was paid more when they lost tournaments than the women's team was paid when they won.

Throughout 2020, many games were canceled due to the worldwide COVID-19 pandemic. Even the Olympic

A LOW BLOW

In 2020 lawyers for US Soccer made a shocking claim. They said science proved the female athletes on the USWNT were inferior to male athletes. The players were outraged, and US Soccer fired the lawyers.

Megan Rapinoe (*right*) runs with the ball during the Tokyo Olympic Games.

Games were postponed. But the team got some good news late that year. New leadership at US Soccer was eager to work with the players and treat them more fairly. The organization wanted a better relationship with the women's team. And the team wanted that too. In November they reached an agreement that would give the women's team the same working conditions and travel accommodations the men had.

In 2021 the team walked away from the Olympics with its first bronze medal. The following February they scored an even bigger win. In a settlement with US Soccer, the federation agreed to pay the players $24 million, which would pay back players who had been underpaid for years. US Soccer pledged to equalize the pay between the women's team and the men's team, and in May it happened. The players got new agreements that guaranteed them equal pay.

The players were ecstatic. Sauerbrunn called all that they had won—including equality in training, playing, and pay—a historic achievement. Foudy said it set a new global standard for women.

"It's a glorious day, and I don't think just for women's soccer," Foudy said. "I think it has so much more meaning beyond women's sports."

The team had won on and off the field and scored a victory for future generations of female athletes.

IMPORTANT DATES

1950   Seventy women join The Craig Club Girls Soccer League.

1972   Title IX is passed, prohibiting discrimination based on sex in schools and other federally funded programs.

1982   The NCAA starts Division 1 women's soccer.

1985   The US Women's National Soccer Team is formed.

1991   They win the first FIFA women's tournament.

1996   The team wins gold at the Atlanta Olympics.

1999   The team wins the Women's World Cup.

2000   April Heinrichs becomes the USWNT's first female coach.

They win silver at the Olympics.

2004 The USWNT wins gold at the Olympics.

2012 The team wins gold again at the Olympics.

2015 The team wins the Women's World Cup for the first time since 1999.

2016 Five top players file a lawsuit demanding equal pay.

2019 The team wins their fourth Women's World Cup.

2022 The team wins their fight for equal pay.

SOURCE NOTES

12 Caitlin Murray, "The National Team: The Inside Story of the Women Who Changed Soccer," Subway Reads, accessed November 16, 2022, https://subwayreads.org/book/the-national -team-the-inside-story-of-the-women-who-changed-soccer/.

13 Murray.

16 Ken Shulman, "'Let's Move On This': The '99 U.S. Women's National Team's Fight for Equality," WBUR, June 7, 2019, https://www.wbur.org/onlyagame/2019/06/07/lilly-foudy -lockout-world-cup-team-usa.

16 Murray.

17 John Walters, "How the First USWNT in 1985 Paved the Way for Women in Soccer," *Sports Illustrated*, June 15, 2022, https:// www.si.com/soccer/2022/06/15/first-uswnt-1985-debut-kim -wyant-linda-gancitano-title-ix.

17 Murray.

19 Karen Price, "Before 1999, the 1996 U.S. Olympic Women's Soccer Team Set the Foundation," Team USA, March 20, 2019, https://www.teamusa.org/News/2019/March/20/The-1996-US -Olympic-Womens-Soccer-Team-Set-The-Foundation.

20 Shulman.

23 Anne M. Peterson, "History Repeats: US Women's Soccer Team Still in Wage Fight," AP, April 17, 2016, https://apnews.com/arti cle/10df9310269c4d808e65637b7996a70e.

24 Jere Longman, "Soccer; 1999 Women's World Cup: Beautiful Game Takes Flight," *New York Times*, May 20, 1999, https:// www.nytimes.com/1999/05/20/sports/soccer-1999-women-s -world-cup-beautiful-game-takes-flight.html.

24 Murray.

25 Longman.

30 Associated Press, "U.S. Women Will Be Paid as Much as Men," *ESPN*, February 2, 2000, https://www.espn.com/soccer/news /2000/0130/325121.html.

31 Jere Longman, "Sydney 2000: Soccer; After a Wild, Intense Match, Norway Steals One from U.S.," *New York Times*, September 29, 2000, https://www.nytimes.com/2000/09/29 /sports/sydney-2000-soccer-after-a-wild-intense-match-norway -steals-one-from-us.html.

34 Andrew Das, "How U.S. Soccer and Its Players Got to Equal Pay: A Timeline," *New York Times*, February 25, 2022, https://www .nytimes.com/explain/2022/02/25/sports/uswnt-soccer-equal-pay.

35 Andrew Das, "U.S. Women's Soccer Players Renew Their Fight for Equal Pay," *New York Times*, July 7, 2016, https://www .nytimes.com/2016/07/08/sports/soccer/us-womens-soccer -players-renew-their-fight-for-equal-pay.html?searchResult Position=10.

36–37 Andrew Das, "U.S. Women's Team Restructures Union in Effort to Revive C.B.A. Talks," *New York Times*, February 3, 2017, https://www.nytimes.com/2017/02/03/sports/soccer/us-women -union-cba-talks-equal-pay.html.

39 "U.S. Women Soccer Players Reach $24 Million Settlement in Fight for Equal Pay," YouTube video, 6:24, posted by PBS NewsHour, February 22, 2022, https://www.youtube.com /watch?time_continue=90&tv=8GwdG2qunIY&feature=emb_logo.

SELECTED BIBLIOGRAPHY

Longman, Jere. "Soccer; 1999 Women's World Cup: Beautiful Game Takes Flight." *New York Times*, May 20, 1999. https://www.nytimes .com/1999/05/20/sports/soccer-1999-women-s-world-cup-beautiful -game-takes-flight.html.

Murray, Caitlin. "The National Team: The Inside Story of the Women Who Changed Soccer." Subway Reads. Accessed November 16, 2022. https://subwayreads.org/book/the-national-team-the-inside-story-of -the-women-who-changed-soccer/.

Peterson, Anne M. "History Repeats: US Women's Soccer Team Still in Wage Fight." AP, April 17, 2016. https://apnews.com/article/10df9310 269c4d808e65637b7996a70e.

Price, Karen. "Before 1999, the 1996 U.S. Olympic Women's Soccer Team Set the Foundation." Team USA, March 20, 2019. https://www .teamusa.org/News/2019/March/20/The-1996-US-Olympic-Womens -Soccer-Team-Set-The-Foundation.

Shulman, Ken. "'Let's Move On This:' The '99 U.S. Women's National Team's Fight for Equality." WBUR, June 8, 2019. https://www.wbur .org/onlyagame/2019/06/07/lilly-foudy-lockout-world-cup-team-usa.

"USA: Clinton Meets Women's Soccer World Cup Winners." YouTube video, 2:05. Posted by AP Archive, July 21, 2015. https://www .youtube.com/watch?v=GLVt3UB9F5Q.

"U.S. Women Will Be Paid as Much as Men." *ESPN*, February 2, 2000. https://www.espn.com/soccer/news/2000/0130/325121.html.

Walters, John. "How the First USWNT in 1985 Paved the Way for Women in Soccer." *Sports Illustrated*, June 15, 2022. https://www.si.com/soccer/2022/06/15/first-uswnt-1985-debut-kim-wyant-linda-gancitano-title-ix.

Ward, Bill. "U.S. Women's Team Settles In at Facility." *Tampa (FL) Tribune*, February 26, 1995. https://www.newspapers.com/image/339825484/?clipping_id=33002099&tfcfToken=eyJhbGciOiJIUzI1NiIs InR5cCI6IkpXVCJ9.eyJmcmVlLXZpZXctaWQiOjMzOTgyNTQ4 NCwiaWF0IjoxNjY3NTY0NzkxLCJleHAiOjE2Njc2NTExOTF9. JejX5xGJCl_SO4Tbo3M-fHzOQkmpp1kQRFjm4To2gNw.

LEARN MORE

FIFA Women's World Cup
    https://www.fifa.com/tournaments/womens/womensworldcup

Loh, Stefanie. *Who Is Megan Rapinoe?* New York: Penguin Workshop,
    2023.

Olympics
    https://olympics.com/en/

Scheff, Matt. *The World Cup: Soccer's Greatest Tournament.*
    Minneapolis: Lerner Publications, 2021.

Skinner, J. E. *U.S. Women's National Soccer Team.* Ann Arbor, MI:
    Cherry Lake, 2019.

US Women's National Team
    https://www.ussoccer.com/teams/uswnt

INDEX

PHOTO ACKNOWLEDGMENTS

AP Photo/Jeffrey McWhorter, p. 2; Marcio Machado/Getty Images, p. 6; Marc Atkins/Getty Images, p. 8; AP Photo, p. 10; Tony Duffy/Getty Images, p. 11; Getty Images, p. 13; Will and Deni McIntyre/Getty Images, p. 14; Bob Thomas/Getty Images, pp. 16, 19, 21; Simon Bruty/Allsport/Getty Images, p. 18; Robert Beck/Sports Illustrated/Getty Images, p. 22, 26, 27; Doug Pensinger/Allsport/Getty Images, p. 29; AFP via Getty Images, p. 31; Wally Skalij/Los Angeles Times/Getty Images, p. 32; Julian Finney/Getty Images, p. 33; Vaughn Ridley/EMPICS/Getty Images, p. 34; AP Photo/Jessica Hill, p. 36; Elsa/Getty Images, p. 38.

Front cover: Sport Press Photo/Alamy Stock Photo.